Only Kidding!

My First Book of Jewish Jokes

Sari Kopitnikoff

Ideastrator Press

Only Kidding!
My First Book of Jewish Jokes

Copyright ©2022 by Sari Kopitnikoff

All rights reserved. No part of this book may be reproduced or used in any manner without written permission of the author except for the use of quotations in a review or article.

ISBN 979-8-9851605-3-6, paperback

Published by Ideastrator Press, New Jersey

The author welcomes feedback at sari@thatjewishmoment.com.

*For my brother Dovid,
who always makes me laugh,
often at the worst times :)*

Contents

Acknowledgments	2
Ha!	3
Terms to Know	4
The Jokes:	
The Jewish Calendar	8
Celebrate	12
Mitzvot and Values	16
Food, Food, Food	20
Holy Things	24
Hebrew Letters	28
At the Door	32
Rejected Jokes	40
Your Turn	44
About the Author	46

Acknowledgments

Thank you so much to the following educators, editors, and jokesters who helped me tweak and develop this book in the best of ways:

Sharon Acierno, Shlomo Aronoff, Bobbi Yael Antonazzi, Melanie Berman, Lisa Bernstein, Julie Blair, Orly Campbell, Julie Friedman, Cheryl Cash-Linietsky, Arnie Draiman, Sarah Friedman, Stacey Gay, Jeremy Katz, Jodi Kaufman, Emily Lieberman, Karen Lilienfeld, Ahuvah Loewenthal, Melissa Puius, Joanna Rubin, Rich Sieger, Dory (and Ellery!) Sangerman, Nati Stern, Beth Tassinari, Sue Weiner, and Erica Yadlovker.

And thank you to my family, friends, and students for laughing at my jokes (or at least pretending to).

Ha!

Welcome to the world of Jewish humor.

It's never too early to begin sharing Jewish puns and riddles.

The pages that follow contain riddles, jokes, and whatnot. Each riddle answer is printed upside down. See if you can guess it before flipping the book over to see what it says. If you can get it, hurray! You're on the way to becoming a Jewish comedian. And if you don't know the answer, no worries: seek to understand it so you can try the joke on your friends and family.

Note: The illustrations on each page do not contain the answers; they sometimes contain hints, and they're sometimes there just to make you smile.

This book is only the beginning. If you start thinking like a comedian, you may soon have notebooks filled with your own original Jewish jokes.

As long as your audience is laughing—or groaning—you're off to a good start!

Terms to Know:

I know, I know. The glossary usually comes at the end of a book. But for you to understand and appreciate the jokes in this book, it's a good idea to look through this list of Hebrew and Yiddish (and even some English!) terms below, and get to know any that are unfamiliar to you. (Note: Some words have multiple pronunciations, so you may need to play around with how you read some of the words to fully appreciate the punchlines.):

Baal Tokeah - the one who blows the *shofar* on Rosh Hashanah

Bar Mitzvah - a celebration when a boy comes of age according to Jewish practice

Bat Mitzvah - a celebration when a girl comes of age according to Jewish practice

Bentch - the Yiddish word for bless; usually refers to making blessings after food

Challah - a loaf of bread, often braided, eaten on *Shabbat* and Jewish holidays

Chametz - A food product that is not kosher for Passover (made from barley, rye, oats, wheat, or spelt)

Chanukah - Hanukkah

Dreidel - a four-sided top spun on Chanukah with the Hebrew letters *Nun, Gimmel, Hey,* and *Shin/Peh*

Hamantashen - a jam-filled pastry eaten on *Purim*

Herring - a kind of fish commonly eaten in some Jewish communities

Ketubah - a Jewish marriage contract

Kiddush - a blessing said over grape juice or wine on special Jewish occasions

Kippah - a beanie or skullcap often worn by Jewish people

Latke - a pancake fried in oil

Maror - Bitter herbs (often horseradish) eaten during the Passover *Seder*

Matzah - A flatbread often made *chametz*-free for Passover

Mazel Tov - A Hebrew expression of congratulations

Megillah - scroll

Mezuzah - a holy parchment attached to doorposts in Jewish homes and buildings

Mitzvah - a commandment, often used to mean a good deed (plural: *Mitzvot)*

Purim - a festive Jewish holiday involving costumes, the exchange of food gifts, giving *tzeddakah*, and reading the story of Esther

Pushke - a container for storing charity

Rosh Chodesh - the beginning of each month on the Hebrew calendar

Seder - the festive meal on the first night(s) of Passover

Shabbat - the Jewish day of rest, from sundown on Friday till nightfall on Saturday

Shofar - a ram's horn blown on Rosh Hashanah

Siddur - prayer book

Siyum - a celebration when one completes studying a part of Torah and other Jewish texts

Sukkot - huts, and the name of the week-long Jewish holiday involving such huts

Tallit - prayer shawl

Tefillah - prayer

Tefillin - black leather boxes and straps wrapped around one's head and arm during weekday prayer

Teshuvah - doing better, making improvements after wrongdoing

Tzeddakah - charity, giving to those in need

Yarmulke - the Yiddish word for *kippah*

The Hebrew letters: *Aleph, Bet, Vet, Gimel, Dalet, Hey, Vav, Zayin, Chet, Tet, Yud, Kaf, Chaf, Lamed, Mem, Nun, Samech, Ayin, Peh, Feh, Tsadi, Qof, Resh, Shin, Sin, Tav*

The Jewish Calendar

Q: What does a baby goat drink grape juice out of on *Shabbat*?

A: A *kid-dish* cup

Q: What's a Jewish bug's favorite day of the month?

A: Roach Chodesh

Q: Why couldn't the congregants hear the *Baal Tokeah*?

A: He was standing shofar away

Q: What keeps you warm on a cold autumn day?

A: Su-coat

Knock knock

    Who's there?

Purim

    Purim who?

Purim me a glass of grape juice please!

Celebrate!

Q: What does a flying mammal celebrate when it becomes an adult?

A: A bat mitzvah

Q: What does a dog celebrate when it comes of age?

A: A bark mitzvah

Q: What's the best musical instrument to bring to a Jewish wedding?

A: A ke-tuba

Q: What do you wish someone upon completing a tricky obstacle course successfully?

A: Maze-l Tov!

Q: What did the student say to the Torah book after many years apart?

A: Long time no siyum

Mitzvot and Values

Q: Why did the Jewish athlete take a seat after eating?

A: To bentch

Q: What did one *yarmulke* secret agent say to another?

A: "*Kippah* an eye on things."

Q: What do you call it when toilet paper says, "I'm sorry"?

A: Tissue-va

Q: Why was the hand crying during *tefillah*?

A: It wasn't *tefillin* so good.

Q: What do Jewish birds do with their extra cash?

A: They give it to tze-duck-ah

Food, Food, Food

Q: How much do potatoes like *Chanukah*?

A: They like it a latke!

Q: What did one hungry *matzah* ball say to the other at the Seder?

A: "Passover a spoon, please."

Q: What did the baker say to the *challah* dough?

A: "I knead you."

Q: Why was the woman worried at the kosher fish market?

A: She couldn't find her-ring.

Knock knock

Who's there?

Boo

Boo who?

Boo Haman, and eat *Hamantashen*!

Holy Things

Q: What do you hang on the entrance of a Jewish zoo?

A: A me-zoo-zah

Q: How do *Megillahs* wake each other?

A: "Scroll, up!"

Q: Why do lots of parents use mini prayer books when they go out?

A: Because they need a baby siddur.

Q: How do you fix a prayer shawl if it's too short?

A: You tall-it

Q: What did the pair of elephants say when they got to the front of the synagogue?

A: "Oops! Wrong ark!"

By the Letter

Q: What do you call it when you steal a *shin*'s dot and move it somewhere else?

A: That's a sin!

Q: Why did the last Hebrew letter wear a smiley t-shirt?

A: So as not to seem too Tav

Q: Do any Hebrew letters come after *mem*?

A: Nun

Q: Why did the Hebrew word go to the doctor?

A: It had a kaf.

Q: What do you say when you suddenly meet a Hebrew letter?

A: Hey!

At the Door

Don't use bell if you're here for a knock knock joke.

Knock Knock

    Who's there?

Noah

    Noah who?

Noah rabbi around here?

Note: To make the jokes work best in this section, you may have to adjust the way you pronounce some of these names.

Knock Knock

    Who's there?

Sarah

    Sarah who?

Sarah kosher store in this town?

Knock Knock

    Who's there?

Chaim

    Chaim who?

Chaim glad to meet you!

Knock Knock

    Who's there?

Leah

    Leah who?

Leah mat at your door!

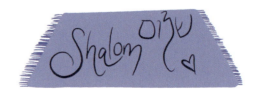

Knock Knock

    Who's there?

Eitan

    Eitan who?

Eitan of us are here, actually!

Knock Knock

    Who's there?

Maya

    Maya who?

Mayan the right block?

Knock Knock

    Who's there?

Ori

    Ori who?

Oreally? Someone's home?

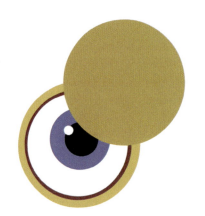

Knock Knock

    Who's there?

Chava

    Chava who?

Chava happy *Chanukah*!

Knock Knock

Who's there?

Talia

Talia who?

Talia neighbors their music is too loud.

Knock Knock

Who's there?

Asher

Asher who?

Asher a fence with you and wanted to say hi.

Knock Knock

> Who's there?

Ezra

> Ezra who?

Ezra way to get to the synagogue from here?

Knock Knock

> Who's there?

Daniel

> Daniel who?

Daniel! You'll wake everybody up!

Knock Knock

> Who's there?

Esther

> Esther who?

Esther anymore hummus?

Knock Knock

> Who's there?

Shai

> Shai who?

Shai come back later?

Did you ever hear the joke about *chametz*?

Never mind, it's kind of crummy.

Did you ever hear the joke about the *kippah*?

Never mind, it'll go over your head.

Did you ever hear the joke about *maror*?

Never mind, it's going to make you cry.

Did you ever hear the joke about the *dreidel*?

Never mind, it's going to make you dizzy.

Did you ever hear the joke about the blintzes?

Never mind, it's too cheesy.

Did you ever hear the joke about the pig?

Never mind, it's not kosher.

Did you ever hear the joke about the moldy cream cheese and lox?

Never mind, I don't think it should be spread.

Did you ever hear the joke about the empty *pushke*?

Never mind, there's no sense.

Did you ever hear the joke about Esther?

Never mind, it's a whole *megillah*.

Your Turn

And now, I challenge you to come up with your own Jewish jokes!

Think about some Jewish holidays, items, and foods, or think of some Hebrew words you know. See if you can put your own Jewish joke together. Say the words aloud, and think about what they may sound like.

If you come up with something good, please share it! Have a parent/guardian send your joke to me by submitting it on www.thatjewishmoment.com.

Keep on laughing,

    Sari

Joke Ideas:

_____

_____

_____

_____

_____

_____

_____

_____

About the Author

Sari Kopitnikoff has been collecting and reading joke books since she was a kid, and she was excited to finally write her own!

Sari is an experiential educator, digital artist, educational performer, and content creator. She is passionate about creating books, games, activities, shows, virtual challenges, and interactive workshops that bring Judaism to life.

You can follow Sari's work on Instagram, Facebook, and TikTok @ThatJewishMoment, and you can find lots of free Jewish educational materials at ThatJewishMoment.com. There, you can book Sari for a live or virtual workshop, sign up for her newsletter, or just say hi.

Other books by Sari:

That Jewish Moment
My Davening Diary
Jewmagine That!
My Escape from Egypt

Made in the USA
Middletown, DE
02 January 2025